Up, Up, and Away!
A Toddler's Flight Adventure

Author: Lia Tuso
Illustrated by: Nafeesa Arshad

Copyright © 2024 - Lia Tuso

All rights reserved. No part of this publication may be reproduced, distributed, or transmitted in any form or by any means, including photocopying, recording, or other electronic or mechanical methods, without the prior written permission of the publisher, except in the case of brief quotations embodied in critical reviews and certain other noncommercial uses permitted by copyright law.

To all the incredible caregivers who choose to explore the world with their Littles,
Who brave the journeys, big and small,
And muscle through the challenge of lugging those car seats along—
Thank you for your unwavering dedication to safety,
For your adventurous spirit,
And for creating memories that will last a lifetime.
This book is for you.

In a bright and sunny town, not far away,

A boy named Santino was ready to play.

His bags were packed, his shoes tied tight,

For today was the day he'd take his first flight.

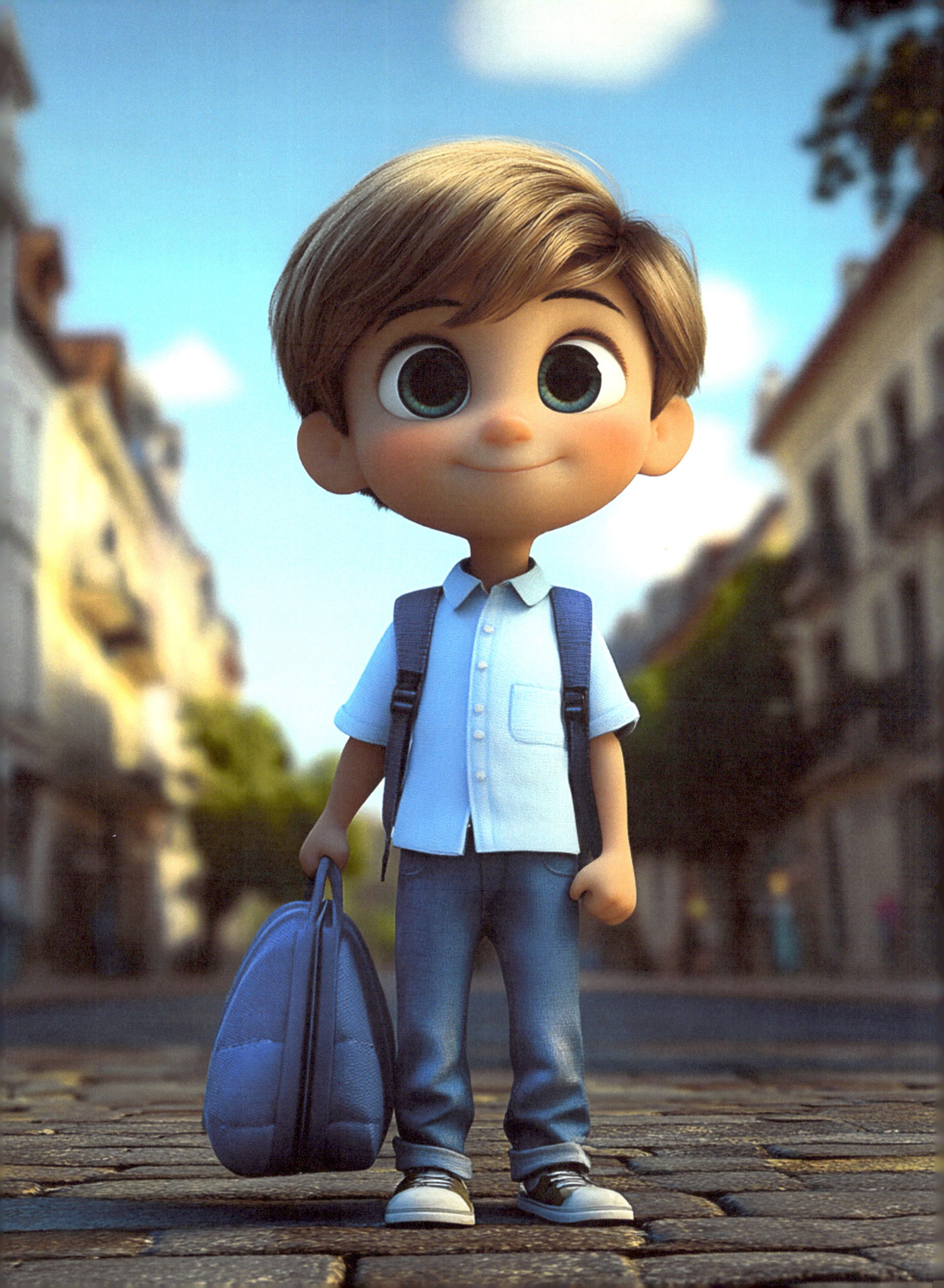

With Mom and Dad by his side,
Santino felt excited, eyes open wide.
They reached the airport, big and grand,
Holding tight to Mommy's hand.

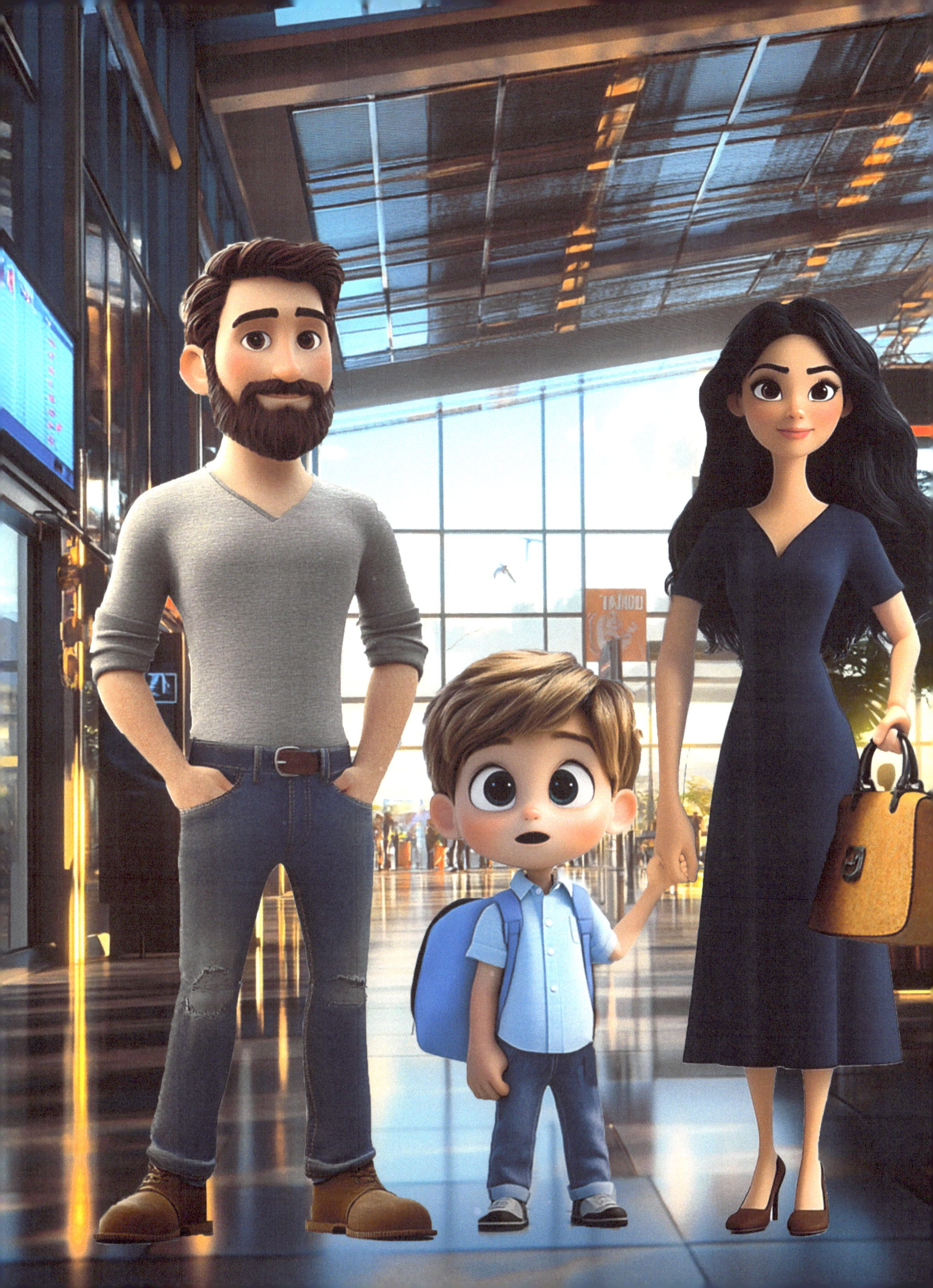

They passed through security, quick as a flash,
Thanks to TSA, they made a dash.
The airplanes outside were big and tall,
Santino couldn't wait to see them all.

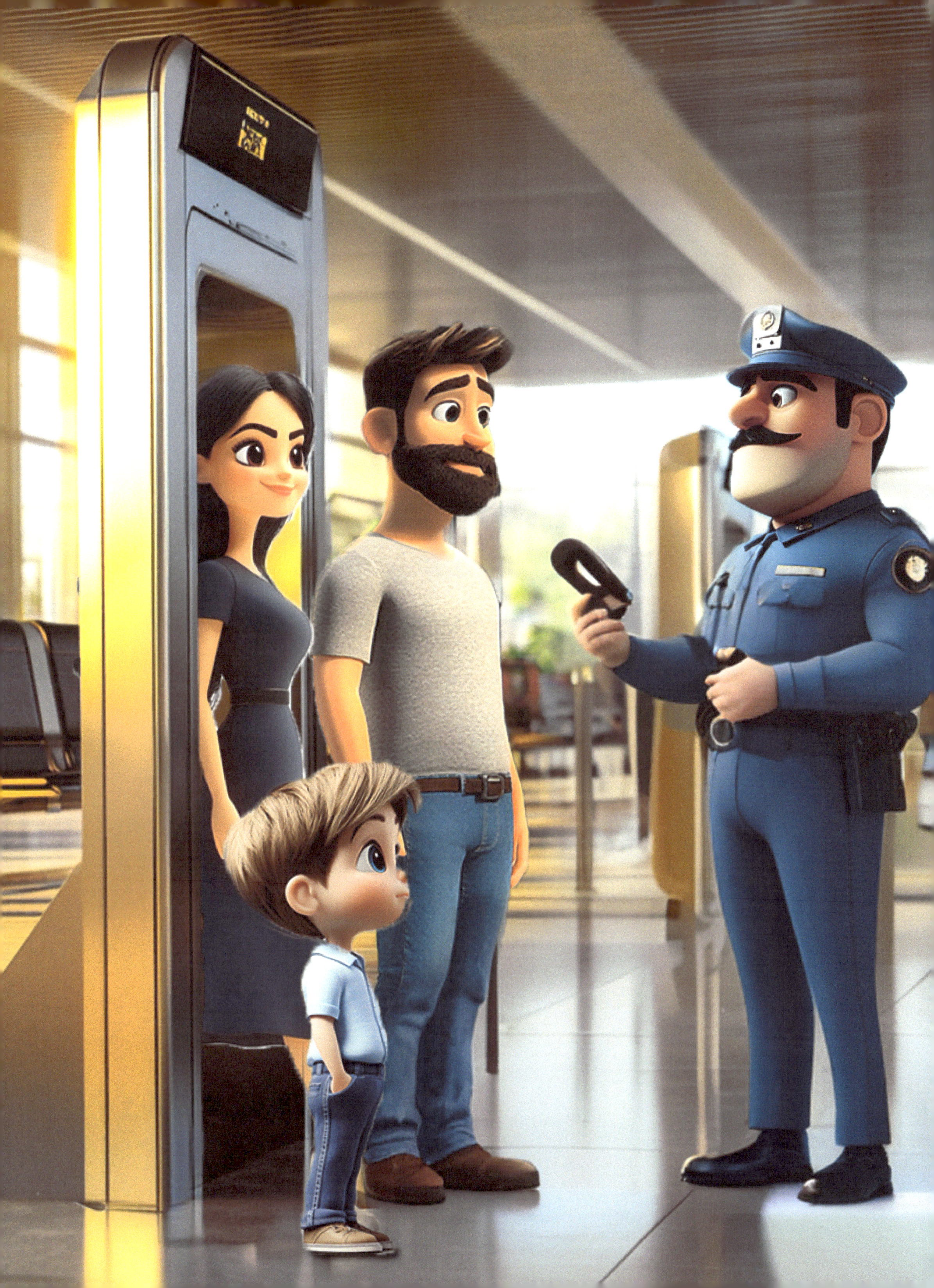

"Time to board!" the gate agent said,
Santino's heart was full of joy, not dread.
They found their seats, row twenty-two,
Mom and Dad knew just what to do.

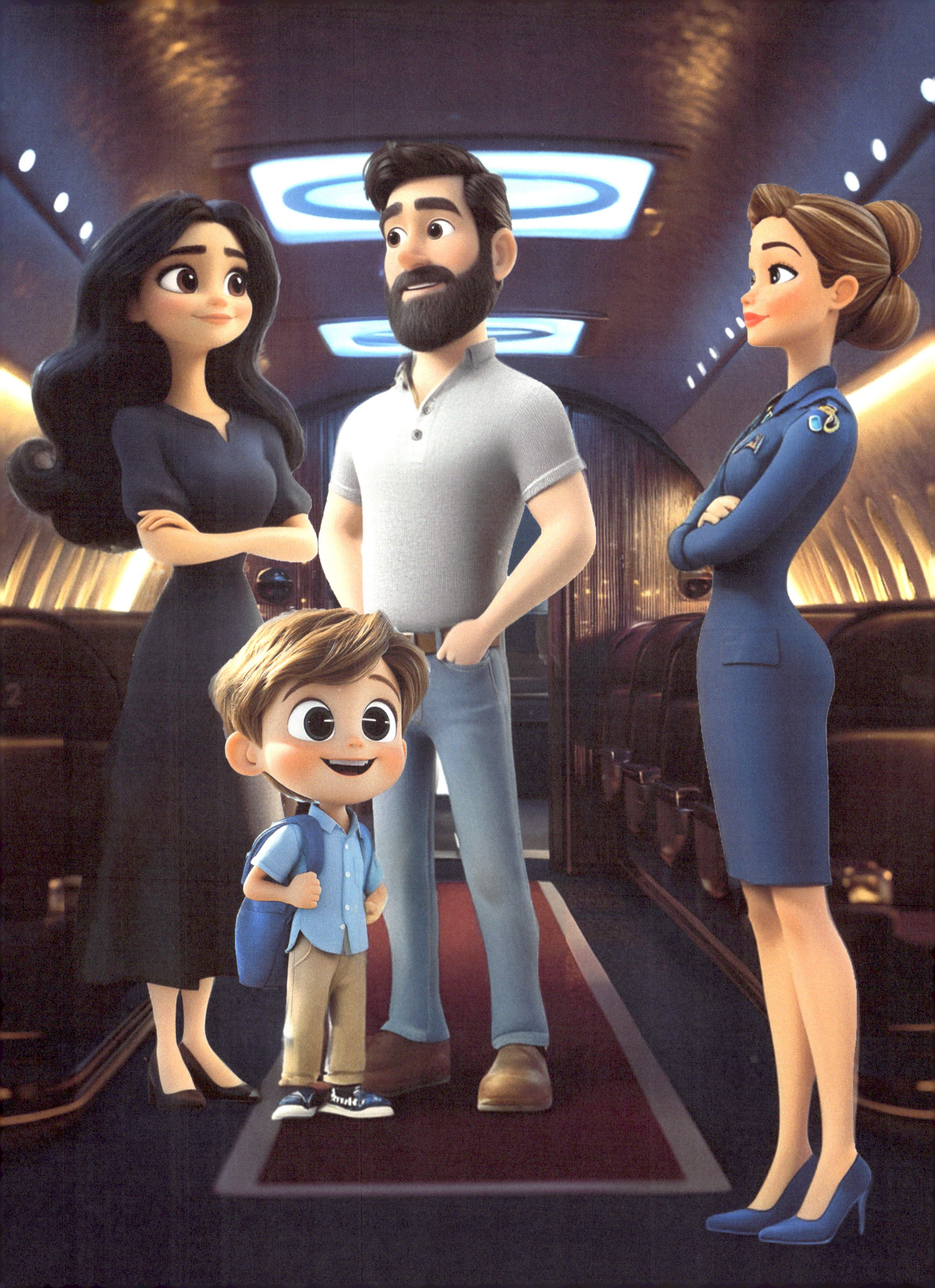

Santino's special car seat was ready and snug,
Mom buckled him in with a gentle tug.
"For safety, Santino, this is the way,
To keep you secure throughout the day."

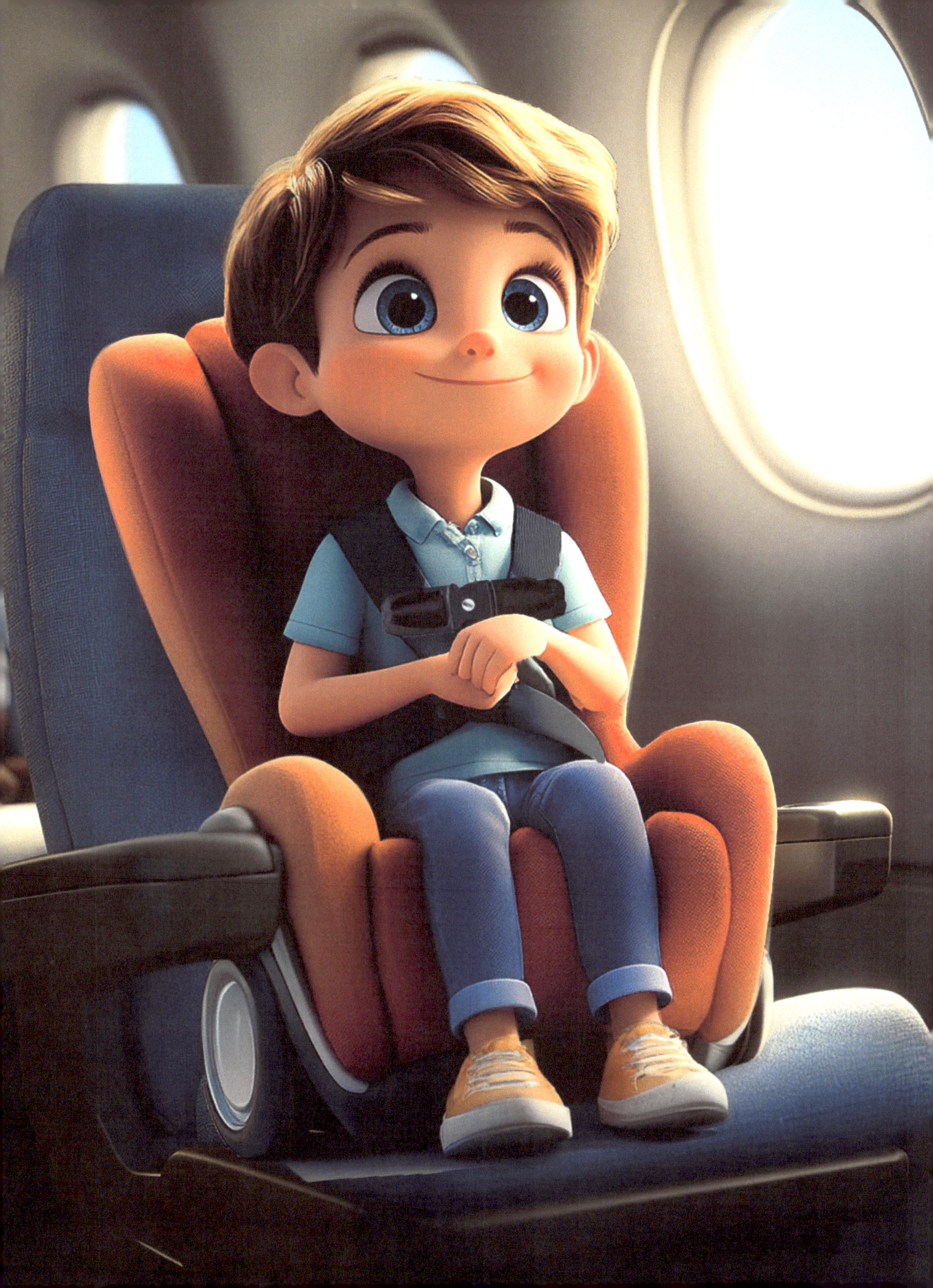

The engines roared, the plane took flight,
Santino looked out with pure delight.
Up, up, up in the sky so high,
They soared like birds, through the sky.

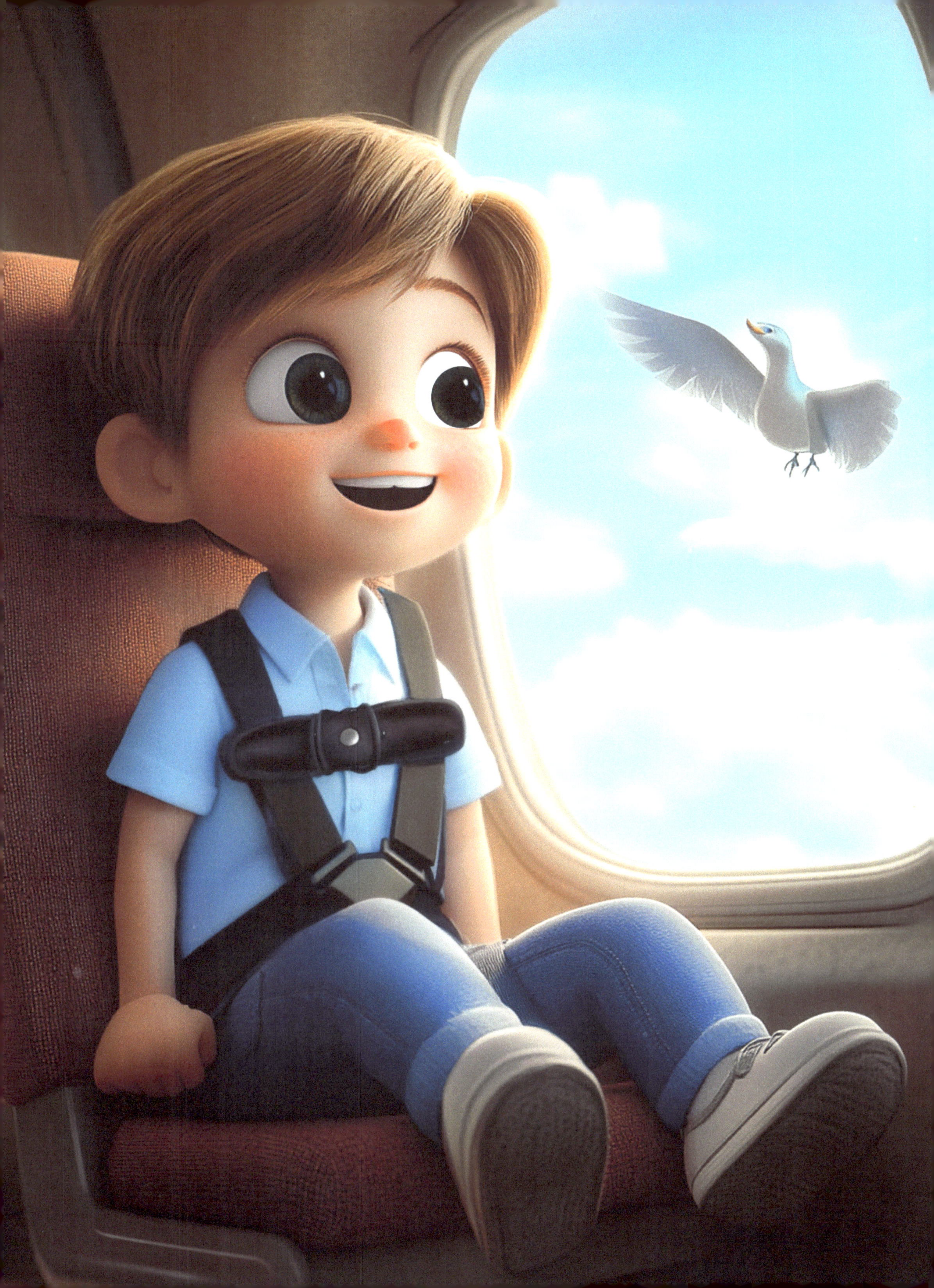

Through the window, clouds so white,
Santino saw the world from a great height.
He munched on snacks, played with toys,
A flying adventure full of joys.

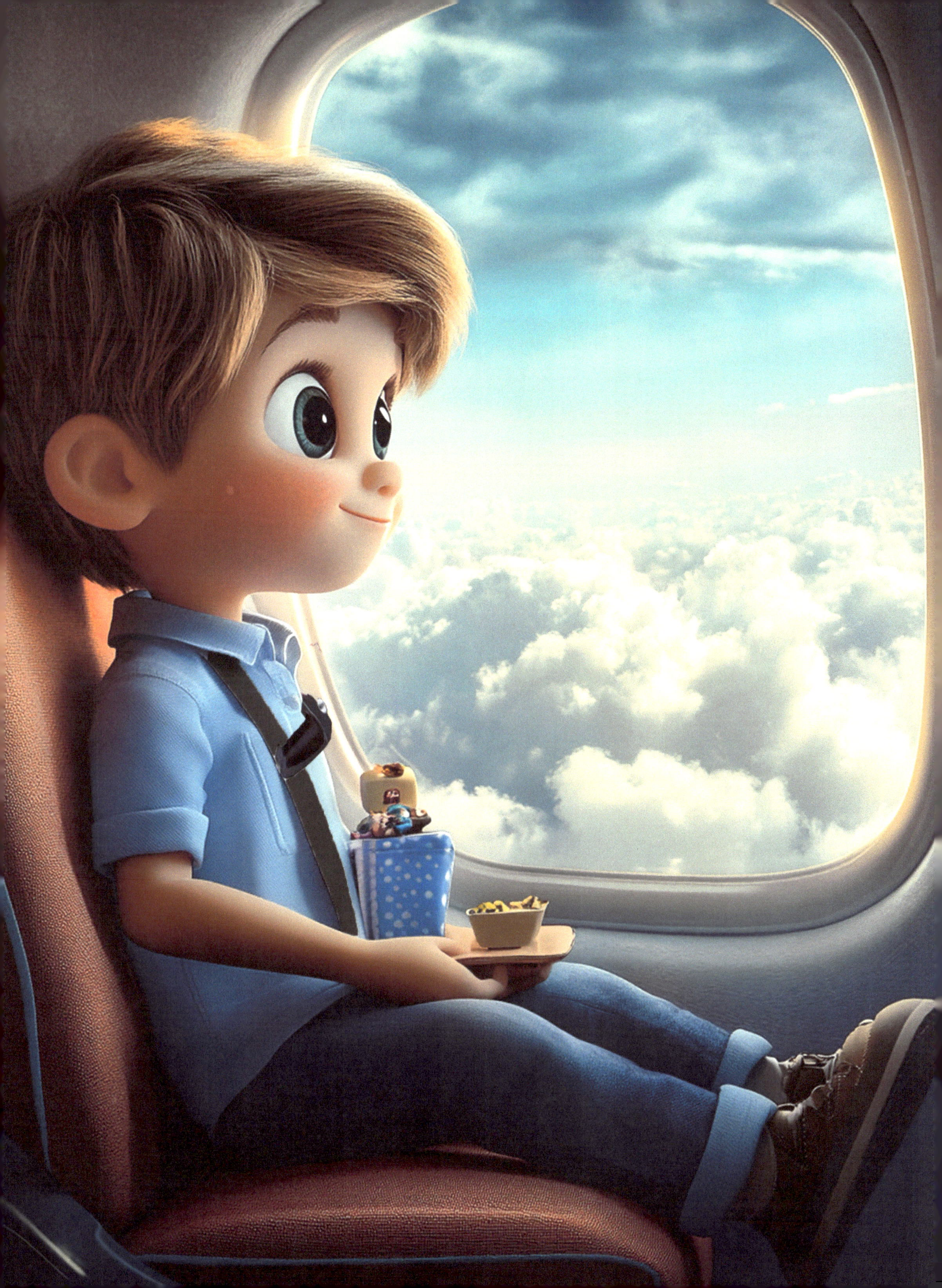

Mom read stories, Dad sang songs,
The flight didn't seem very long.
Santino felt safe in his car seat,
Traveling in the sky was such a treat.

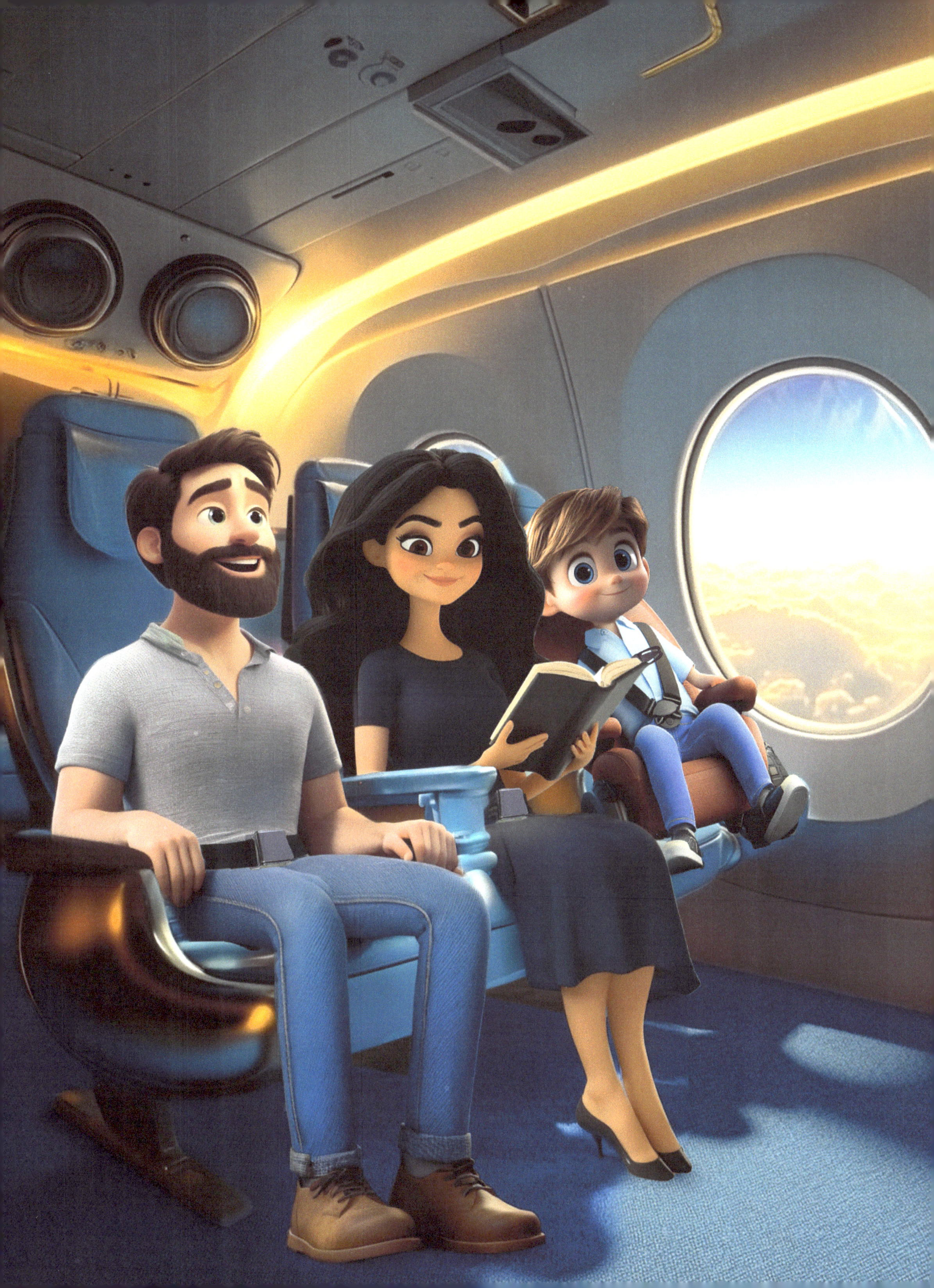

"Look, Santino, we're almost there,"
Mom pointed with loving care.
The plane descended, landing smooth,
Santino felt calm, in a happy soothe.

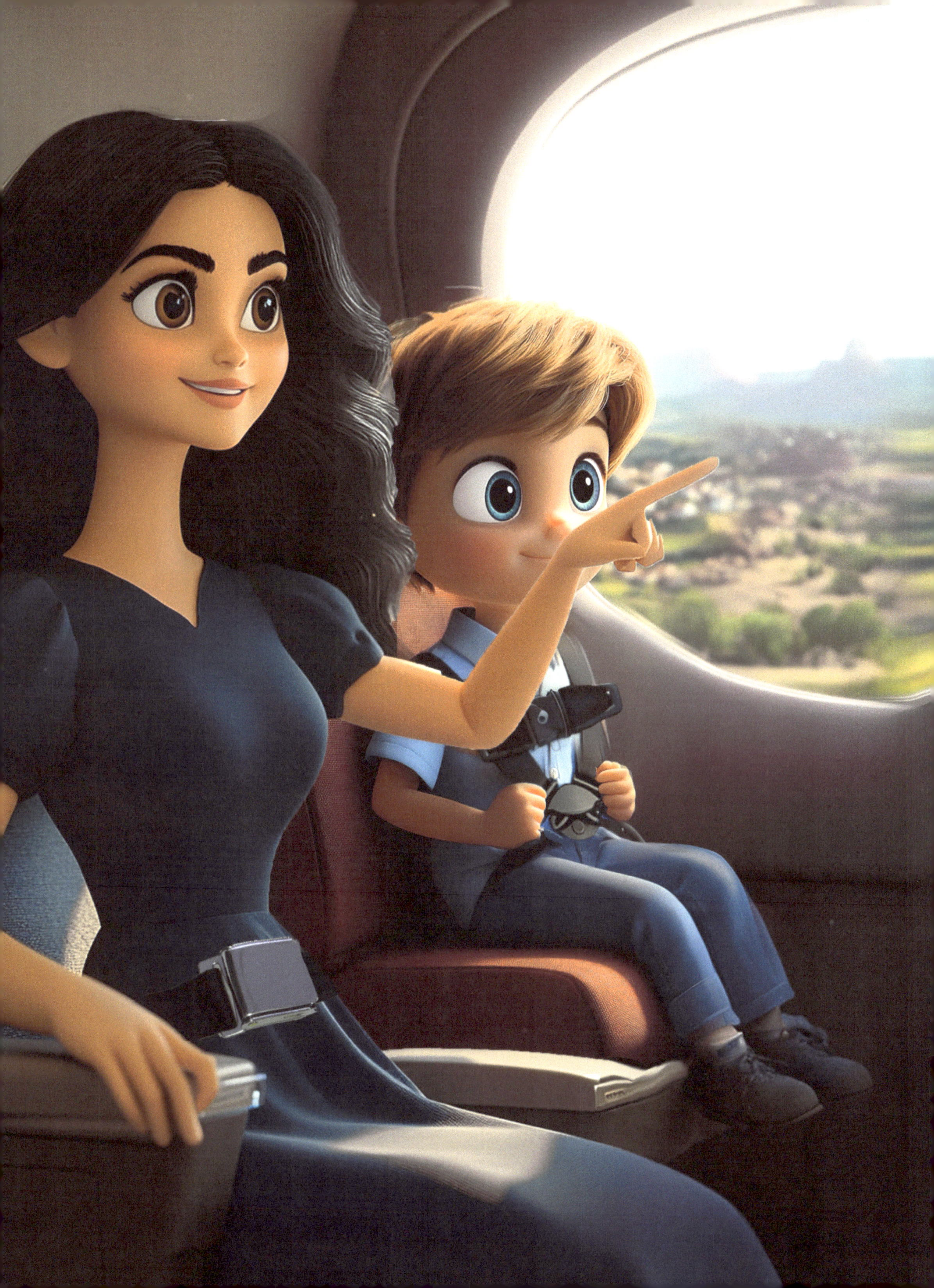

Unbuckled from his car seat tight,
Santino knew he had traveled right.
Down the aisle, with tiny feet,
Ready to explore, new people to meet.

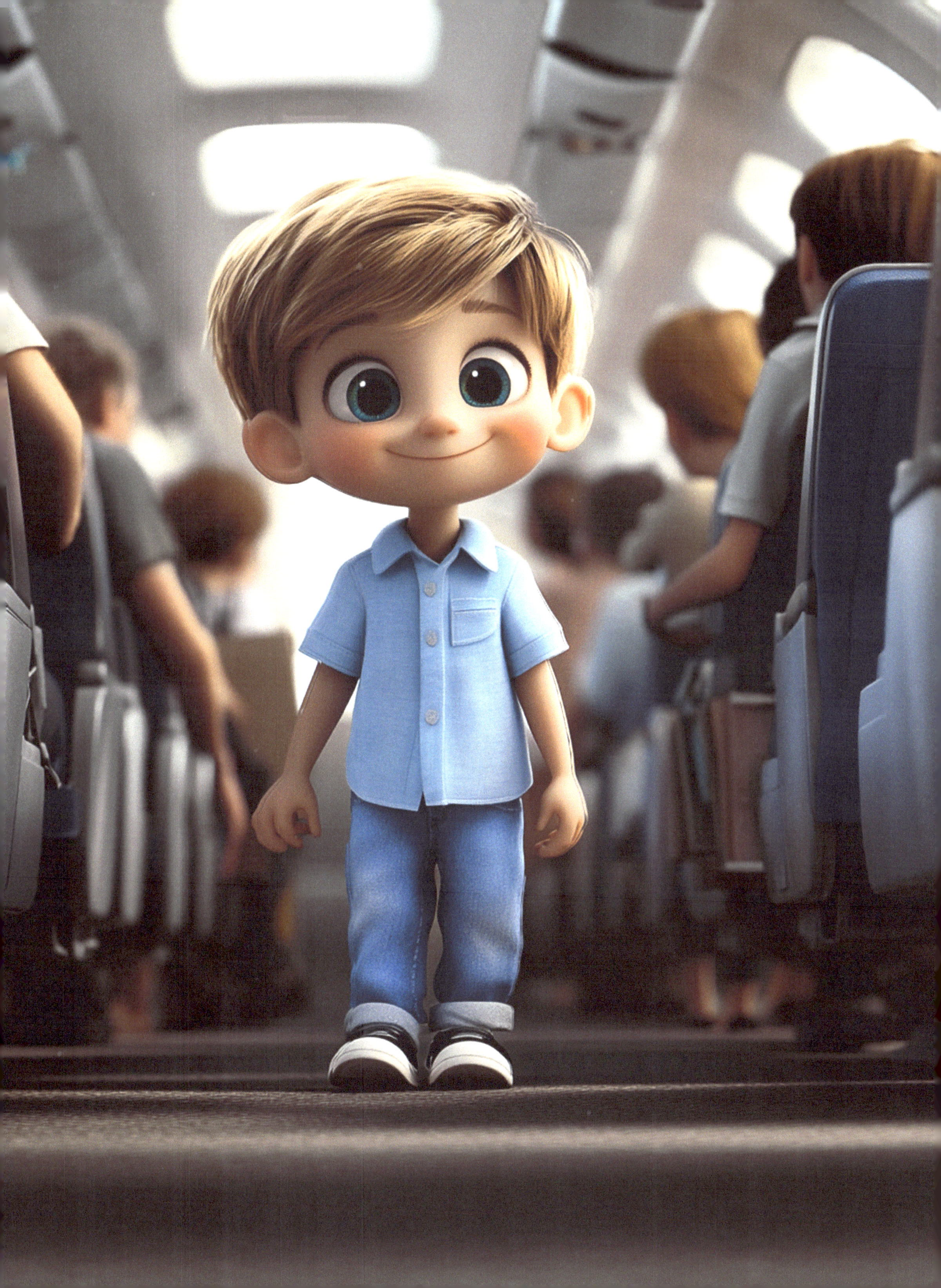

They stepped off the plane, feeling grand,

Mom and Dad each holding a hand.

Santino saw new places, faces so kind,

The joy of travel, he would soon find.

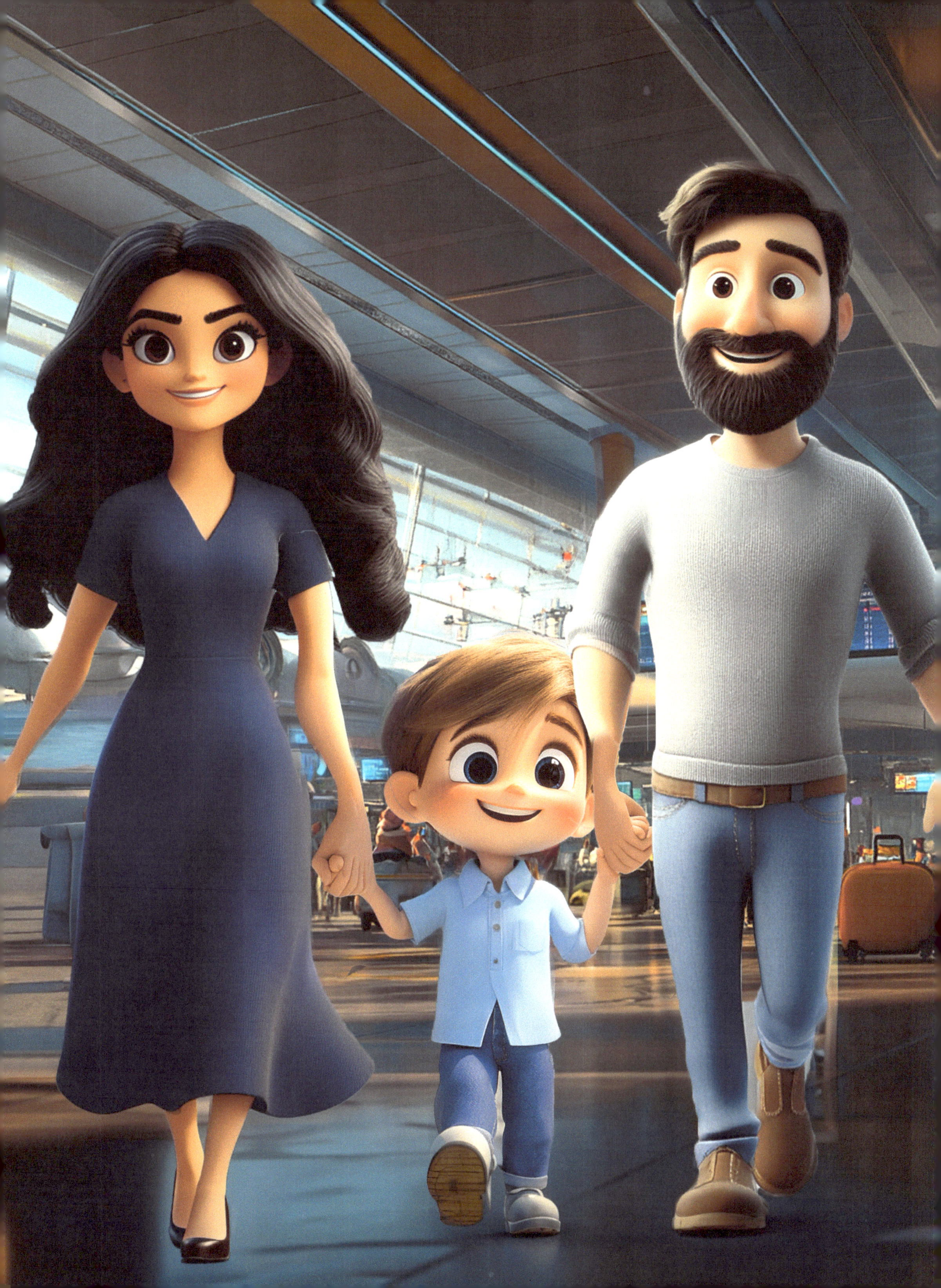

With Nonni and Papa waiting, arms open wide,

Santino ran to them, filled with pride.

Hugs and kisses, love all around,

A safe and happy flight, with adventures abound.

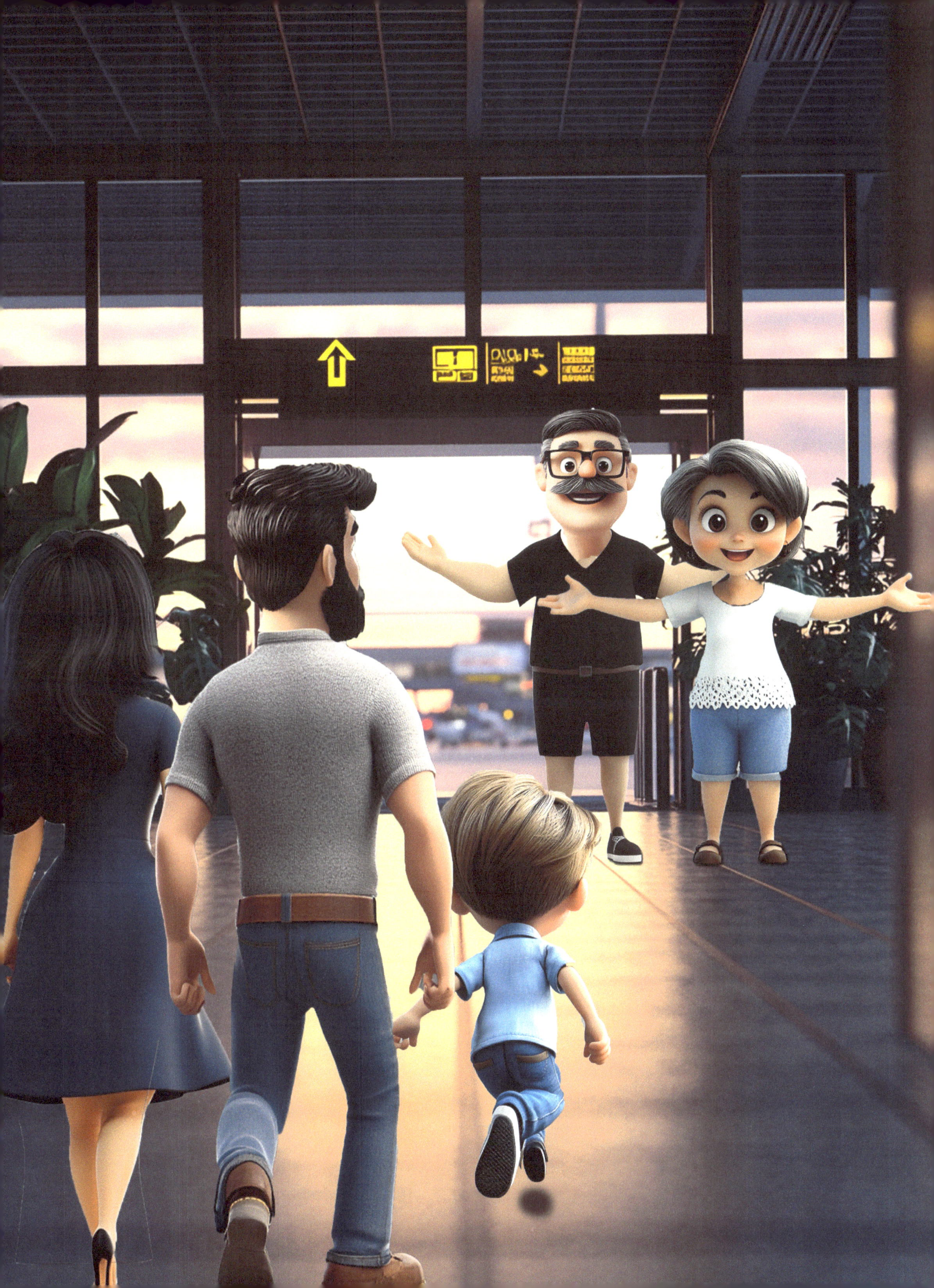

Santino learned that day, in the sky so blue,

That flying safely was fun and true.

With his special seat, and parents near,

Every journey was nothing to fear.

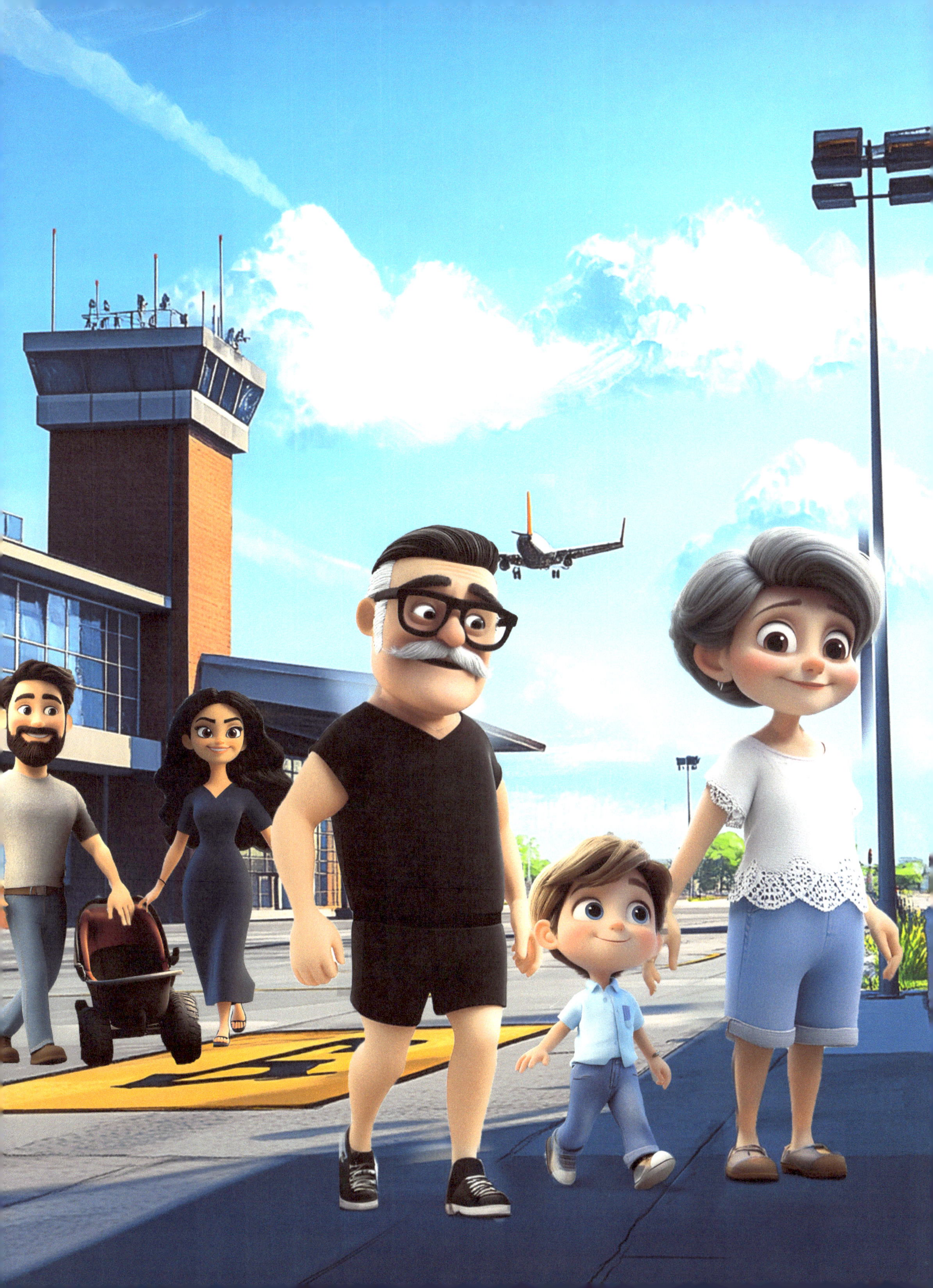

So remember, little ones, wherever you go,
Buckle up tight, and take it slow.
For safety is key, in the air or on the ground,
With love and adventure, joy will be found.

Printed in the USA
CPSIA information can be obtained
at www.ICGtesting.com
LVHW071708161024
793945LV00007B/105